Epic Adventures

Written by Tony Bradman
Illustrated by Roger Simo

Contents

Meet the Adventurers

This book is about two men who liked to have adventures.

Name: Christopher Columbus
Job: sailor and explorer

They lived at different times and had very different adventures.

Name: Neil Armstrong
Job: jet pilot and astronaut

Where Were They Going?

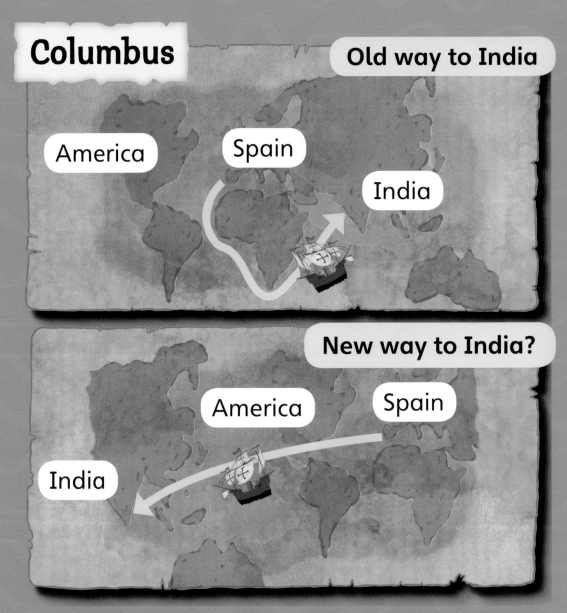

Columbus **Old way to India**

America

Spain

India

New way to India?

America

Spain

India

Christopher Columbus's journey started over 500 years ago! He wanted to find a new way to sail from Spain to India.

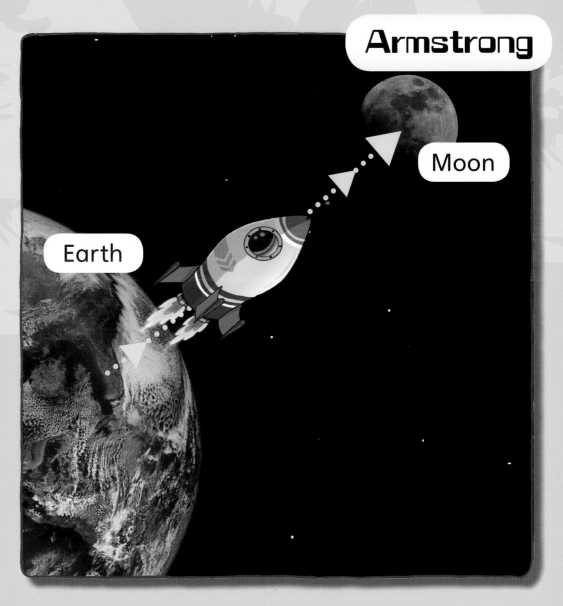

Neil Armstrong's journey started over
50 years ago. He wanted to fly from Earth
to the Moon. No one had ever landed there!

How Did They Get There?

Columbus

Columbus travelled in a ship called the *Santa Maria*. It sailed on the sea.

Armstrong

Armstrong travelled in a spaceship called *Apollo II*. It flew in space.

What Did They Take With Them?

Columbus took lots of food and drink on his journey.

Columbus

fish

water

salted meat

He also took chickens on the ship so the sailors could eat them!

Armstrong took food for his journey too.

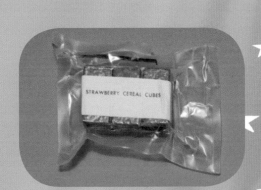

Armstrong

space food

He also took his scout badge
to remind him of home.

What Were Their Journeys Like?

Christopher Columbus sailed for five weeks on the sea. He was looking for a place to land.

Columbus

His ship almost sank and he ran out of food and water.

Neil Armstrong flew for just one week to get to the Moon and back to Earth.

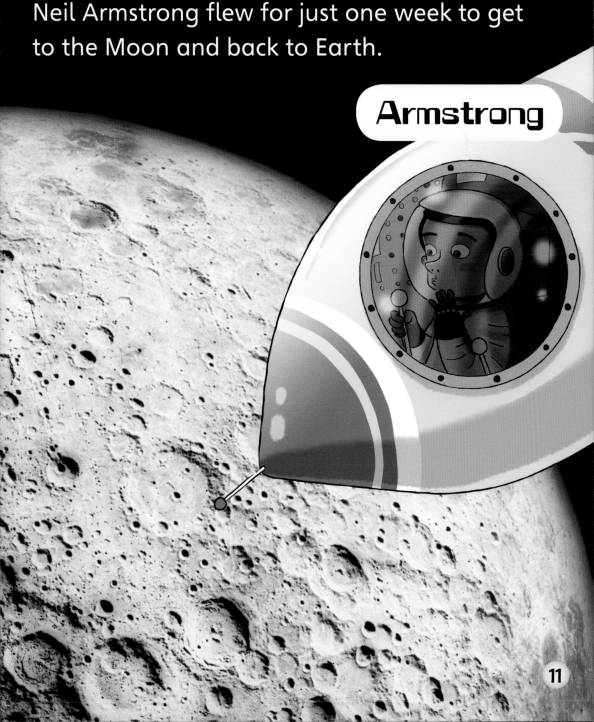

Armstrong

Where Did They Go?

Columbus

Columbus did not land in India. He landed in a new place. It was near America.

Armstrong

Armstrong landed his spaceship on the Moon.
He could see all of Earth!

What Did They Find?

Columbus found foods he had never seen!
He took lots of new food home in his ship.

Armstrong

Armstrong found rocks and dust on the Moon.
He took some moon rock back to Earth.

Index